How Does It Feel When Your Parents Get Divorced?

Books by Terry Berger

HOW DOES IT FEEL WHEN YOUR PARENTS
    GET DIVORCED?

I HAVE FEELINGS

BLACK FAIRY TALES

How Does It Feel When Your Parents Get Divorced?

By TERRY BERGER

Photographs by Miriam Shapiro

JULIAN MESSNER NEW YORK

Sixth Printing, 1981

JULIAN MESSNER and colophon are trademarks of
Simon & Schuster, registered in the U.S. Patent
and Trademark Office.

Text Copyright © 1977 by Terry Berger
Photographs Copyright © 1977 by Miriam Shapiro

Printed in the United States of America

Design by Marjorie Zaum

Library of Congress Cataloging in Publication Data

   Berger, Terry.
      How does it feel when your parents get divorced?

      SUMMARY: Discusses problems and emotions
   young people experience when parents divorce, the
   family separates, and life styles change.
      1. Children of divorced parents—Juvenile
   literature. 2. Divorce—Juvenile literature.
   [1. Divorce] I. Shapiro, Miriam. II. Title.
   HQ777.5.B47   301.42'84   77-332
   ISBN 0-671-32883-2

For
Susan and David—*who know*

ACKNOWLEDGMENT

I am grateful to Dr. Julius Rice, Great Neck, Long Island, psychiatrist and author of *Ups and Downs*, as well as to Dr. Sheldon Golub, chief psychiatrist of a children's clinic, and to his staff, for reading the manuscript in light of their professional expertise.

T.B.

How Does It Feel When Your Parents Get Divorced?

How does it feel when your parents get divorced?

I can tell you. I know.

My parents were divorced—
almost two years ago.

Before my parents got divorced,
they used to fight all the time.
They'd argue about everything, and yell.
Sometimes they didn't speak to each other for days.

I felt scared.

Would they stop talking to each other forever?
Why didn't they like each other any more?
Would they stop liking me?

When my parents talked about getting divorced,
I thought I was to blame.
Lots of times I annoyed them.
And I spoiled their fun when I got sick.

I felt guilty.

I tried to be good by being quiet
and doing whatever they told me.
I gave them a plant for their anniversary,
and brought them breakfast in bed.
They still kept fighting.
They said they were not fighting about me.

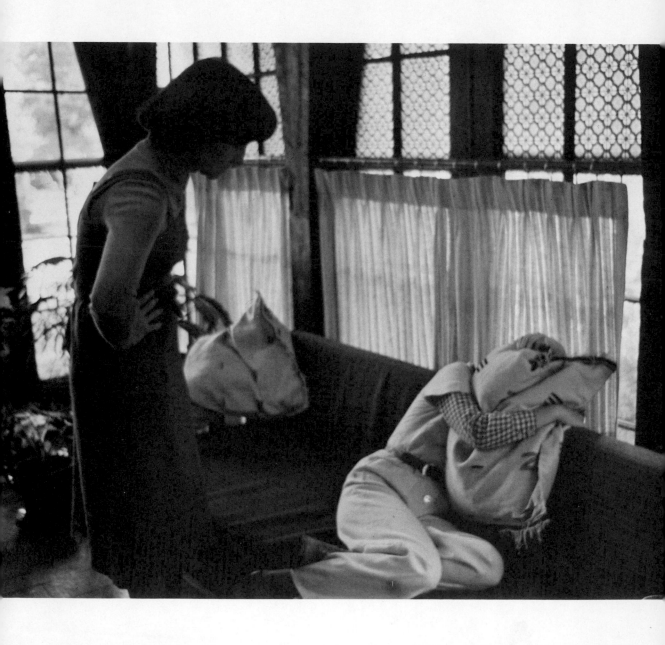

Sometimes my Mom said bad things about my Dad.
And my Dad said bad things about my Mom.
My Mom said my Dad was a liar.
My Dad said my Mom was stupid.

I couldn't stand listening to either one.

I didn't want to hear them say bad things
about each other.
I loved them both.

Then my parents decided to get divorced.
Dad said he would be moving away.
I asked him how could he leave me.
Who would take care of me?
Who would be my Dad?

I felt angry.

I wanted to keep Mom and Dad together.
I needed them.
I loved them.
Why couldn't they love each other?

My Father went off to live by himself.
I cried and begged him to stay.

I felt he didn't love me.

He wasn't around any more when I wanted him.
He used to kiss me good night.
I only saw him on weekends,
and I spoke to him on the phone.
I missed him.

I missed him all the time.
At first, I cried almost every night.
It was hard to fall asleep.
I was angry at Mom for letting Dad leave.

I felt unhappy.

It was awful.
But after a while I didn't cry as much.

The house seemed empty with just Mom and me.

I felt lonely.

Even though Mom spent more time with me,
it was strange not having Dad around.
But the yelling stopped.
And now that they were apart,
Mom and Dad were nicer to be with.

My parents both got lawyers.
My parents were divorced.
They said they were happier that way.

I felt very disappointed.

At first, I pretended my Father would come back
and marry my Mother again.
I would go to the wedding.
He didn't.
It was hard pretending any more.

Now I was alone with my Mother.
What if something happened to her?
Who would take care of me?

I felt worried.

My Mother told me if she couldn't take care of me,
my Father would.
I wonder if he can.

I started doing everything wrong.
I tried getting back at my parents.
If they won't behave, I won't either, I thought.
I stopped doing homework,
and threw my clothes on the floor,
and got into fights with my friends.

I felt mad.

But doing things wrong didn't make things better.
It only made everyone more unhappy—
especially me.

I didn't want the kids in school
to know about the divorce—
that my parents couldn't keep our family together.
I thought something was wrong with us.

I felt ashamed.

But now my friends know.
And they're still my friends.
Anyway, some of them have divorced parents too.

When I realized we were no longer the same family—
that it was no longer me, Mom and Dad—

I felt part of me missing.

I began to understand how much my family meant to me.
And how sad I felt when that changed.
But I guess Mom and Dad are happier.

I started cleaning my room,
and helping Mom shop and cook.
We took care of the house together.

I felt important.

I couldn't take my Father's place.
My Mom can't take his place either.
But Mom and I helped each other more.

Twice when my Dad promised to take me out,
he didn't.

I hated him for that.

Mom said he must have had to work.
It wasn't his fault.
It wasn't mine, either.

The first time I went to my Father's apartment,
it felt strange.
He had a sofa that opened into a bed.
I saw him cleaning and cooking
and sewing on buttons.

I was surprised.

My Mom used to do those things for him.
I never knew Dad could take care of himself.
I'm glad he can.
I think he can take care of me.

My Father told me he was lonely too.
But he was making new friends.
I met some of them.
They talked about things I didn't know.

I felt left out.

Dad reminded me that there were times
when only he and I did things together —
like playing checkers and making up funny stories,
and fishing off the pier.
We couldn't always do things by ourselves.

Almost two years have passed since the divorce.
We had to sell our house.
There was not enough money
to take care of Dad and us.
Mom and I live in an apartment now.

I feel sad.

My Mom goes to work.
She's never home when I get back from school.
But I do my homework and set the table for dinner.
I get along okay.

One evening, a man came to see my Mother,
and took her out on a date.

I felt jealous.

I wanted Mom all to myself,
like she'd been since Dad went away.
But Mom said she needs friends.

47

What if Mom married someone else?
I wonder if I'd like a stepfather?
I wonder if a stepfather would like me?

I'm not sure.

Maybe the stepfather would have his own children.
Some of them might live with us.
I'd have another family to do things with.
But maybe I wouldn't like them.

Sometimes I wonder if I'll ever get married.
I don't know if I want to.
Being married can make people unhappy.

I feel mixed up.

Aunt Lee and Uncle Aaron are happy.
So are Aunt Marilyn and Uncle Sidney.
I guess marriages can be good.

Even though my parents' marriage was not good,
they both care for me.
When I was at camp last summer,
they both came up to see me.

I feel loved.

Although my parents no longer live together,
their feelings for me are the same.

I'm doing more things by myself.
I'm taking pictures,
and I'm learning to play the guitar.
I joined a bowling league.

I feel good.

I started doing things I never did before.
I am learning things.
I am beginning to feel more grown up.

55

Now I spend less time thinking about the divorce.
I spend more time playing with my friends
and having fun.
And thinking about things I want to do.

I feel better.

I can still be happy.

ABOUT THE AUTHOR

TERRY BERGER was born in New York, and grew up there and in Pennsylvania. During her teen-age years, she wrote poetry as well as her first story for children.

She attended Vassar College where she majored in psychology, concentrating on the study of early childhood. Later she taught kindergarten and first grade, during which time she published her first book, *Black Fairy Tales*. It was later recorded, and is included in the Kerlan Collection, a research center for children's books at the University of Minnesota.

I Have Feelings, her next book, was made into a film.

Ms. Berger is divorced, the mother of two children: a son, David, and a daughter, Susan. She and her family have experienced all of the feelings in HOW DOES IT FEEL WHEN YOUR PARENTS GET DIVORCED?

ABOUT THE PHOTOGRAPHER

MIRIAM SHAPIRO says about herself: "I was born in Charleston, South Carolina, and moved to New York City at the age of nineteen, working as a secretary and going to college at night. I was married a year later.

"During the time of my marriage, I became a volunteer at Manhasset's North Shore Hospital, and it was there that I became interested in photography. The hospital had a photo contest each year, and the winning photographs were hung on the walls. As soon as I could, I signed up for a photography course. I bought my first 35M camera, and shot everything in sight. I also joined a camera club, and spent all my free time with the camera, pestering my children and my husband to pose for me. I won several awards for photographs of my son, Howard, and daughter, Leslie.

"By this time I decided to turn my hobby into a profession, and took a photography course at C.W. Post College. Soon I was accepted for shows, and my work was hung with photographers of worth. I have since shown at several galleries, been published in magazines, and have a photograph in the Chase Art Collection.

"Four years ago I was divorced. My children are at college now.

"I want to thank the O'Ferralls, the models in this book, my first one. They are a beautiful family, happy with themselves and each other, willing to pose to help children who read this book understand that the pains of divorce lessen with time and understanding."